# A Beginner's Guide To Taoism

Patrick Stewart

Published by Patrick Stewart, 2023.

# The Taoist Online

[thetaoist.online](http://thetaoist.online)[1]

Copyright @ 2024 Patrick Stewart

All rights reserved.

No part of this book may be reproduced or used in any manner without the prior written permission of the copyright owner, except for the use of brief quotations in a book review.

To request permission, contact the author at patrick@thetaoistonline.org

First e-book edition January, 2024

---

# Table of Contents

To my wife, kids, mother, brothers, and family who have supported me in this crazy adventure called life. I love you all.

And to the editors, writers, and readers of The Taoist Online. Without your advice, encouragement, comments, and claps, I would not have the courage to continue writing.

# Introduction

If you've read my previous work, you might wonder, "Hey, I know who you are."

"Oh, you do?" I'd say in return.

You would say, "You're a writer, poet, community organizer, father, husband, and busy as hell."

All of those are true, yet I am more lost than ever. Perhaps it's the inability to see forward that causes it. If I knew where this was all going, I wouldn't feel so aimless.

As a kid, my parents told me precisely what would happen in my future. I would go to high school and college and then figure out what I should do with my life. I'd pick a job and be happy.

What nonsense! It's not like I've spent my whole life bouncing around, trying to turn one hobby into a career after another.

Oh, wait. Yes, I have.

In high school, I lived and breathed music and theater. I started playing percussion in the sixth grade and was reasonably good compared to the others in school. I was always the second chair to a kid named Michael, my age. However, I joined the top concert, marching, and jazz bands and even played drums for the orchestra during musical theater in my junior and senior years. When it came time for college, it seemed like a no-brainer to continue my musical journey at the University of North Texas, one of the top music schools in the country.

What else was I going to do? It was all I knew, the only thing I seemed to do well and enjoyed.

My friends told me to "go into computers" as if they knew what that phrase meant. I liked playing computer games as much as the next '90s teen and eventually got into building my computers, but a hobby doesn't always become a great career choice.

So, in 2001, I started college at UNT and found my skills were not unique compared to others, but far from bad. I was considered talented, but I could have been more exceptional. After the first semester, I called my mom and wanted to change majors, but she told me to stick it out and that I would adjust and improve. However, I didn't know what to do after two and a half years and thousands of dollars in student loans because my love for music had run out.

What else did I like to do besides music? I liked to talk. I was a great conversationalist to everyone who knew me. My friends, girlfriends, lovers, and parents enjoyed talking to me. A communications degree seemed like an obvious decision.

After all, acting, public speaking, speech writing, logical reasoning, and more came naturally to me due to my time on stage in middle and high school. No one knew I was just bored and lost.

What else was I going to do? It was all I knew, the only thing I seemed to do well and enjoyed.

Another four years went by, and in 2007, I graduated with a degree in Communications with a minor in rhetorical theory. I could talk to you in circles and constantly use it to win arguments with my friends and wife, who refused to engage me in most debates. On the other hand, my brothers still knew how to play me.

After graduating, I again discovered all the skills I had learned amounted to terribly little in the outside world. Interestingly, I looked at job postings and found no one needed a "Good Listener" or "Beginner Level Talker." So, at 25, with my first child on the way, I fell back to my long-lost hobby–computers.

What else was I going to do? It was all I knew, the only thing I seemed to do well and enjoyed.

I landed my dream job at an Apple Store in Fort Worth, and I saw the release of the first few iPhones and even the iPad. Also, I stayed long enough to watch Steve Jobs grow older, become ill with cancer, and die. I worked long hours overnight as a part of the visuals team until 6 a.m. after working a whole shift, all while being part-time for $10 an hour.

Eventually, I was promoted to full-time and climbed the ladder to become a Genius behind the Genius Bar. For those unfamiliar with the term, I was a technician who fixed computers and iPhones. But, after five years, I couldn't stand missing holidays, delaying family get-togethers, or missing my children. I quit Apple in 2013 and moved into Information Technology for a non-profit on their helpdesk team.

After five additional years, now 32 years old, I didn't want to be a helpdesk technician and moved into cloud computing. I bounced around related jobs, working for different online e-learning platforms, and I still do.

A few years ago, nearly 37 years old, I had a cancer scare (which wasn't cancer) that changed my views on life. It caused a shift in my religious, spiritual, and philosophical beliefs. I became heavily involved in Taoist philosophy and ideology, raised three children into their teens, and found my son was special needs.

After everything in my career, family, and life choices, I discovered I had decades of experience I could share. So, I tried to convey the intense emotions I previously kept contained through a newfound desire to write. I wrote poetry and stories in college, but had set that aside for computers. Now, I picked up the practice of writing again and gathered others around me who shared my desire.

What else was I going to do? It was all I knew, the only thing I seemed to do well and enjoyed.

Steve Jobs once said, "You can't connect the dots going forward, only looking backward." But it's hard to connect any dots when I look at my life. I don't see a straight line from point to point like a bird or airplane. Instead, I see a web — a patchwork of train tracks spread throughout the sprawling city of my existence.

There was never a map or a tour guide. I thought about the challenges life presented and made a choice. No book or voice from heaven told me what to do when my 19-year-old girlfriend was pregnant with my kid or what college to attend. What book of the Bible or verse from Tao Te Ching taught me what career I needed to choose? Religion and philosophy didn't answer my questions or give me the answer to life's hardships. However, they did provide me with boundaries.

If I'm a car, and my life is a tangled mess of a highway system (welcome to Dallas), then Taoism is my double yellow line. It's not my Google Maps or GPS since it won't tell me where to go, but it will help me stay on the correct side of the road. Taoism helps me know where I might go. I can look around and see who's on the same side of the road. We don't all have the same destination, but we travel together.

I'm slower now. I make decisions when they arise and never worry about the past. Even looking backward, life isn't always a game of connecting the dots because no one can understand the trillions of actions that caused you to be where you are today.

The story of the Chinese farmer by Alan Watts teaches us that no one can know if an event is good fortune or bad fortune. So, looking back at my own life, I only know that everything I have experienced happened. The circumstances didn't have to occur in the way they did, and I rarely chose a path that did not end in a completely different solution than I planned.

My journey, life, and experiences in the chapters ahead create a picture of my origin, but not a crystal ball of my destination. No one can know their destiny for certain, and your guess is as good as mine as where yours will lead. I do, however, know a single truth I'd like to share.

I am me, and I am going. So, let's get started.

Patrick Stewart

Texas, 2024

# Nature's Powerful Way

## ~ What Is Tao? ~

I am not a scholar or an expert, nor do I consider myself a wise man. Just ask my wife and kids. My friends would say I know enough, though. Most scholars would laugh at me. However, I am a student with a few years under my belt, and even if I cannot answer every question, I can help you start on your path. Together, we can enjoy our journey.

Does it matter if legends are factual or not? Most, I assume, would say no. King Arthur and the Knights of the Round Table is mostly fiction, but the stories continue regardless. Kids run through their yards playing 'Knights,' and attractions like Medieval Times succeed in bringing thousands of people to see their show.

So, too, is the story of Laozi and the creation of the Tao Te Ching, sometimes spelled Dao De Jing. The pronunciation is closer to the latter, but when searching for books or topics, you will find the former as it is the classical spelling. Tao (with a T) was produced by Thomas Francis Wade during the mid-19th century and was given completed form in Herbert A. Giles's Chinese–English Dictionary of 1892. The more modern spelling (with a D) is a part of the Pinyin system created by the Chinese government during the 1950s. Both are considered correct, and you will find books in either spelling.

The most frequently found story of Tao Te Ching's creation goes like this. 2500 years ago, Laozi was a librarian in the imperial archives and had grown tired of daily life's political turmoil and stress. And so, he decided to leave it all behind and travel to the countryside. On his way out of town, he was stopped by the border guard and asked to write some words of wisdom. He wrote a collection of 5,000 words, later divided into eighty-one chapters. Then, having written his thoughts for the guard, he climbed on top of his water buffalo and rode off into the sunset, never to be seen again.

Unlike religions such as Christianity, if Laozi did not exist, the wisdom in the text would still be as relevant, practical, and impactful as it would be if he did exist. Whether it was collected by others over time or written by one person an extraordinarily long time ago, the ability of the text to transform nations, its power to influence people's ideology, and its place in history are unquestionable.

## Tao

The Tao Te Ching is one of the most widely translated book on Earth, second only to the Bible. The title is often translated as "The Book of the Way" and Its Power." Or sometimes referred to as "The book of the way." Tao itself can mean "a way" or "the way."

While metaphorical and poetic, the chapters explain a way of life that is in balance with nature. The Tao itself, I describe as the force behind all creation. Depending on how religious you would like to travel down the Taoism rabbit hole, it can be a god. Still, most westerners, like me, who were raised Christian but did not enjoy being told what to do with our destiny, think of it as the universe's path.

The first line of the Tao Te Ching, when translated by scholar Derek Lin, can be as follows:

*The Tao that can be spoken is not the eternal Tao.*

*The name that can be named is not the eternal name.*

This means that any attempt to describe the Tao itself is folly, and any name we would give it is also useless. Because of this, you will find irony and contradictions everywhere within its eighty-one chapters. However, since our language is word-bound, we must call it something. Therefore, Laozi admittedly chose the word Tao.

## The Wisdom Within

In just eighty-one chapters, Laozi describes how to live life and govern a nation harmoniously with Tao. But why should we? The best answer I can give you might be the story of a man in a river.

One day, a man fell off his boat into a strong river. Knowing he needed to get to shore, he had two choices: swim against the current and attempt to keep his place in the river, or swim with the current and allow it to carry him further away. If the man swims against the current, he faces drowning due to the flow of the water, sticks, and rocks. No matter how hard he swims, he will still flow downstream, just not as far. If he swims with the current, he can certainly reach the shore. Having saved much of his strength, he can build a fire and shelter to spend the night safely.

If you fight the Tao's natural flow and ignore the rushing waves bellowing against you, Laozi believed you would face a much more difficult life filled with struggle, strife, and sadness. If you, however, decided to live in harmony with nature and moved forward with its current, then a much more joyful and peaceful life could be yours.

You have a choice either way. No one will force you to choose one path over the other. No god will punish or reward you for either method. The river is doing what is natural for the river. The rock is doing what a rock does, tumbling in the water with all the fish, plants, and sticks. They do not stress or worry about where they are and do not regret where they have been or what they have lost. They enjoy and are content with where they are now.

As I stated at the start, I am not an expert, and if you are interested, please immerse yourself in Derek Lin's copy of the Tao Te Ching. In fact, it is helpful to find different translations and compare them. Learn from everyone and everything you can.

# The Boy and the Yin-Yang

## ~ How Taoism Found Me ~

Once upon a time, there was a boy who was ten years old. He liked his family's new computer because it had a color screen and a mouse. But most of all, it had a paint program. He loved MS Paint, and during his summer days, he would find national flags, symbols, and logos to draw on Paint. He drew the Texas flag first, which was his home state, then the United States, something called NATO, which seemed easy enough, and China, Russia, and Colorado for his mother. But one day, he found a strange circular symbol with only two colors: black and white. The two colors seemed to be swirling into the center as if neither one could overtake the other. When his big brother came home, the boy asked, "What is this symbol?" His brother replied, "Oh, that's a yin-yang." "What is it for?" asked the boy. "I'm not sure, but I think it means opposites or balance or something," his older brother quickly replied as he walked off. The boy loved this MS Paint picture most of all. He wasn't sure why or where the yin-yang came from or even what it meant, but he liked it deeply. And for many years, he remembered that drawing he created one day in MS Paint.

Fast Forward. The boy is now 19 years old. A fan of Winnie-the-Pooh since before his MS Paint adventure, a friend asked if he had ever heard of a book named "The Tao of Pooh," to which he replied, "No." "I think you would like it," the friend said. The boy looked in the library, but the book was checked out. He also didn't have money since he was a poor college student. He asked his girlfriend to buy it for his birthday, but instead, she bought another Pooh book about business and success. The boy didn't like those books, he read a few pages and never picked them up again.

Fast Forward. The boy is now 37 years old, married, has three kids, two dogs, and possibly testicular cancer. Times are hard. He attends a local arts and jazz festival with his wife to attempt to relax and not stress too much. At the festival, he finds a vendor that sells handmade necklaces made of bone. He notices that one of the necklaces has a yin-yang. The boy remembers using MS Paint all those years ago. He remembers almost buying the Tao of Pooh all those years ago. He remembers that yin-yang has something to do with Taoism, which he had understood from researching the Pooh book. Several months later, he discovered it wasn't cancer but a rare mass of non-cancerous cells, but surgery was still required.

During recovery, the boy began researching this yin-yang he was now wearing. He discovered it was Chinese and could be found in nature. He found an entire sect of Westerners who follow Taoist teachings and philosophy. He discovered Discord servers, websites, YouTubers, and online classes. He read every copy of translated ancient books like the Tao Te Ching and Zhuangzu. He discovered he loved reading for the first time! He read anything he could from anyone, including Alan Watts. He joined online communities, attended classes from George Thompon, and built friendships online, and... it was good. He felt his life had been enriched again, like when he married and had children. New opportunities presented themselves, and new relationships began. Life slowed down, and a calm routine set in.

Fast forward. The boy is now 40 years old. He developed tinnitus and, for the past year, has struggled with anxiety attacks, lack of sleep, and medications that wreak havoc on his meditation, practice, and peace of mind. What was once beautiful peace and quiet had become a high-pitched squeal 24 hours a day, seven days a week, with no breaks...ever. Through many weeks, he was able to gain the upper hand on the condition. Sleeping became a regular occurrence, but the damage had already been done. He left the communities, stopped learning, sat alone in a house, and wondered if peace would find him again.

One day, he joined a new social network called Mastodon. He looked for a Taoist community, but couldn't find one. He rejoined his old Discord server, and discovered the ability to stand up and manage a Mastodon instance wasn't as hard as he thought. There were certainly Taoists on Mastodon, but no instance to call home. He wanted to share his story and everything he had learned. He hoped he could find a different path forward if he shared what he had learned. He knew his journey wasn't over, and he was slowing down. Sharing his thoughts and feelings wouldn't be a miracle cure for anything, and he couldn't promise to help anyone do anything differently.

After all, he remembered drawing the yin-yang on MS Paint all those years ago. If the yin-yang, and thereby the Tao, could speak to, guide, and show itself to him, then perhaps it could do the same for others. They need a place to find it.

And so, with all this in mind, the boy created... The Taoist Online.

# The Uncarved Block

## ~ What It Means To Be Worthless ~

My wife loves puzzles, but I do not. When we were first married, she tried to get me to help put them together. At first, it was a 1,000-piece puzzle. After I said no, she tried five hundred pieces, but I was not budging. She resigned herself to putting it together alone, only to discover she was ONE puzzle piece short. Where did it go? Who knows? The puzzle was now ruined and useless.

But is it useless? What is useless?

In Tao Te Ching, there is a concept called the Uncarved Block. The phrase appears eight times in the text and refers to a person's natural state. Translated from the Chinese character "pǔ" (pronounced like Winnie-the-"Pooh"), it can be defined as the following:

- unworked wood

- cut down, felled trees

- nature; essence; intrinsic quality (compare English in the rough)

- simple; plain; unadorned; unaffected

Left: modern "pǔ". Right: primitive "pǔ."

When looking at your everyday life, you may think you have become a better person — more knowledgeable, smarter, and wiser. But in Taoism, there is a concern we grow further away from our true nature. We lose ourselves as we grow older due to society, work, and other outside forces.

Laozi, the legendary figure credited with the writing Tao Te Ching, recommends the following in chapter 28 (J.H. McDonald, 1996).

*The block of wood is carved into utensils*

*by carving void into the wood.*

*The Master uses the utensils, yet prefers to keep to the block*

*because of its limitless possibilities.*

*Great works do not involve discarding substance.*

For example, when people are born, they are perfectly in tune with nature. Babies do not have words to define their surroundings, yet they know their parents. They cannot hold a conversation, yet they communicate their desires with everyone around them. Anxiety over the future or depression over the past is not possible for them.

These problems are taught to us later in life as we learn our native language.

Here, the baby represents us in our uncarved state — a limitless person whose potential expands to the entire universe. Anything is possible, if given the opportunity, and such potential only decreases with knowledge and age.

Another Chinese philosopher, Zhuangzi, also wrote about the concept of the uncarved block. Zhuangzi lived sometime before 286 BCE. Unlike Laozi, most scholars believe Zhuangzi existed and credit him for his work. A humorous and quick-witted writer, some readers prefer his storytelling method to the philosophical poetry of Laozi.

One of my favorite stories Zhuangzi wrote is the following:

*Huizi said to Zhuangzi, "This old tree is so crooked and rough that it is useless for lumber. In the same way, your teachings have no practical use!"*

*Zhuangzi replied, "This tree may be useless as lumber, but you could rest in the gentle shade of its big branches or admire its rustic character. It only seems useless to you because you want to turn it into something else and do not know how to appreciate it for what it is. My teachings are like this."*

As is so perfectly explained, nothing is useless. Every object can be utilized, but our cultural and personal ability to define the world around us limits our expectations and actions. For example, in Zhuangzi's story, the tree will not make a serviceable boat, table, or chair because the wood is too crooked and rough. But Huizi failed to see the tree as useful since he only thought about what it could become.

For three years, if you were a Tao-Zen Exchange Discord server member, you might have seen the screenname "The_Uncarved" in chat. I love the concept of the uncarved block so much that I used it as my username! Growing up with a famous first and last name (Patrick Stewart), I didn't want those stereotypes following me into a new community. I wanted people to see who I was from my words and actions and not who I had been because of a silly coincidence with my name. Sometimes, we must unlearn our lessons to see the true nature of our surroundings. Even when what we must forget is who we have become.

---

*When we lose ourselves, we find ourselves.*

---

# Wu Wei: Non-Action

## ~ How To Live Your Life Without Trying ~

"You're in tune with everything that's going on. You control the tempo, you control everything. It's like you can do anything." — Michael Jordan, 1992.

No professional athlete knows what it is like to be "in the zone" better than Michael Jordan: multiple 50 points games and even 60 points games. When asked what it is like to play those kinds of games by Playboy in 1992, Jordan stated the quote above. He would go on to describe that it seemed effortless. He could do everything and anything he wanted, and it always worked.

And it isn't just Michael Jordan who has noticed this phenomenon. Search for any dominating professional athlete, and they will tell you the same thing. It almost feels like they are not even trying. It's action without effort. A natural, automatic state-of-being flows from them, which allows them to perform incredible feats, and they don't even think about what action they're performing.

However, you do not have to be a professional athlete to experience effortless action. Have you ever concentrated on an activity so hard that everything in your mind disappears?

How about during sex? What makes good sex? Is it when you are mentally switched on that nothing else in the world seems to matter except for your body?

If you have ever been so focused that everything else fades away, you lived Wu Wei.

---

*Wu Wei is the practice of taking no action that is not in accord with the natural course of the universe.*

---

How do we know that the action is in accord with the natural course of the universe, you ask? When you do not think about it and when it flows out of you without having to concentrate actively. The significant part about Wu Wei is that it can happen more often than you think.

Here is an exercise you can perform to help you live Wu Wei.

In his book The Miracle of Mindfulness, Tich Naut Han tells a story about when he was washing dishes at a friend's house. In it, he states that when you clean the dishes, only think about cleaning the dishes. Do not think about anything else but doing the dishes. So let your day fade from your mind, and concentrate on each dish, plate, or bowl. Listen to the running water drown the noise of life away.

In my house, we divide chores between my wife and I. Dishes are my chore five days a week, but I love it! Over the past year, I have noticed a few things about the task.

1.  The sound matches the pitch of my tinnitus and helps relieve the stress of the ringing.
2.  If I am worried about the day or regretful about yesterday, those emotions fade away too.

This result did not come quickly; it takes daily practice, but you can get there with any action. After enough exercise, you can live your entire day this way! Please do not think that I am a master at it, but I am a pretty good dishwasher.

# Ten Thousand Things and the Creation of the Universe

If you read any English translation of the Tao Te Ching, the ancient Chinese seminal text of Taoism, you have read the phrase "10,000 things." How strange! In fact, you will occasionally find the exact phrase in Buddhist texts as well. So, what are these things, and how did we get here?

To answer those questions, we need to understand the Tao. But, you see, you cannot understand the Tao. You are not supposed to. The first line of the first chapter of the Tao Te Ching ensures you know that you cannot understand the Tao.

*The Tao that can be told is not the eternal Tao.*

This statement means that anything you can say about the Tao is incorrect. Words are incapable of describing it. If you are lost or confused so far, then you understand perfectly.

Taoism is wrapped in paradoxical and contradictory language because we are attempting to put into words that which cannot be put into words.

*So how, then, are we supposed to understand what the 10,000 things are if we can't talk about Tao or even know what it is?*

Luckily, the legendary author, Laozi, has an answer... **with words!**

# Chapter 42

We may not be able to understand what Tao is technically, but we can see the ramifications of its existence—its manifestations. In other words, we can see what has occurred due to Tao in the real world. For example, in his third law of motion, Sir Isaac Newton put it this way.

*Every action has an equal and opposite reaction.*

If one action occurs, another MUST also arise. We will come back to this phrase later.

Halfway through Tao Te Ching, in chapter 42, Laozi writes the following:

*The Tao gives birth to one.*

*One gives birth to two.*

*Two gives birth to three.*

*And three gives birth to the ten thousand things.*

*The ten thousand things carry yin and embrace yang.*

*They achieve harmony by combining these forces.*

It is here that we find the answer to the unanswerable question. In it, we find the creation of the universe, Earth, animals, and humanity. How is this possible, you ask? You see, these two stanzas describe the yin and yang.

Everyone is familiar with the yin-yang symbol. You see it on t-shirts, bumper stickers on cars, tattoos, and necklaces. Yes, I have a yin-yang necklace, but more on that later. Most people think it stands for balance or opposites. The Taoist meaning is more complicated (because, of course, it is, right?). Let me explain.

## The Meaning

To understand the true meaning and discover what the 10,000 things are, let us read chapter 42 one line at a time.

---

*The Tao gives birth to one.*

---

We start with Tao. Many followers believe Tao is a god, and if that is your interpretation, you're welcome to it. In my mind, however, it is not a god or a deity but a force with no form. So, if you are thinking about Star Wars, keep going with that thought because you are getting there. From nothing, one, the universe, is born.

*One gives birth to two.*

From the universe, a system of duality appears naturally. Remember, for every action, there is a reaction. For everything, there is the opposite thing. Two **IS** yin and yang. They are opposing but equal forces in the universe–male and female, strong and weak, beautiful and ugly. You cannot have one without the other, and they coexist perfectly. So, they were created at the same time.

It is crucially important that you understand the parts of **two** cannot survive without each other, or else it would not be **two**. It is not **yin** and **yang**; it is **yin-yang**.

*Two gives birth to three*

When we usually see a yin-yang, it is stationary like the picture above or perhaps a pendant. But the two halves of yin-yang rotate, forever challenging each other and pushing the other out of the way. This push of yin causes yang to move yin to the side. This spin cannot stop, or it would not be yin and yang anymore. It would be **one.**

*This constant movement, the dance that never ends, the interaction, is three.*

*Three gives birth to the 10,000 things.*

So, remember Sir Isaac Newton's third law of motion? The cosmic reaction to yin and yang constantly spinning and interacting is the existence of **everything**.

*The ancient Chinese called this concept 10,000 things.*

## The Final Picture

On April 27th, 2019, I promised never to feel again as lost as I felt that year. Not that I have not felt stress, anxiety, or had medical problems afterwards, but I dedicated myself to learning as much about the Tao as I could. It was not long before I began to identify openly as a Taoist.

So, on the same day, April 27th, since 2018, I take a selfie and attach it to the right side of this collage.

Sometimes, my friends and family ask what my necklace means to me. While I have given different answers over the years, my favorite is...

*Everything.*

# Why This Pattern Everywhere in Nature?

The yin-yang is more than you can possibly imagine but easy to understand.

Everybody knows the yin-yang. You can travel to countries worldwide, and people will tell you they at least recognize the pattern — black turns into white, white turns into black, some back in white, some white in black. It nearly sounds like a Dr. Seuss rhyme, but it's as real as you and me.

In my research, the yin-yang is older than recorded history. So, we won't ever discover who created the pattern originally. My Taoism teacher, George, has a theory of how it was created, however. It involves the golden ratio.

The pattern is clear throughout nature, from the tiny disk flowers in the middle of a sunflower to the medium-sized conch shell to the gigantic arms of a spiral galaxy. In fact, different cultures discovered the same pattern through mathematics.

The golden ratio, often written as the Greek letter phi ($\phi$), has been studied since at least 300 BCE in ancient Greece. This means different cultures from different parts of the ancient world noticed the same shapes and patterns in nature early in recorded human history. How can this pattern appear in so many living things, yet all life is completely random? What is it about the fabric and the foundation of life that continues to create this pattern?

The first chapter of the seminal book of Taoist philosophy, Tao Te Ching, states we don't know the answer to that question and never will. Confused? Don't worry. Let's take a look.

---

*The Tao that can be told is not the eternal Tao.*

*The name that can be named is not the eternal name.*

*The nameless is the beginning of heaven and earth.*

*The named is the mother of ten thousand things.*

*Ever desireless, one can see the mystery.*

*Ever desiring, one can see the manifestations.*

*These two spring from the same source but differ in name;*

*this appears as darkness.*

*Darkness within darkness.*

*The gate to all mystery.*

---

If I told you I could explain the chapter above perfectly, I'd be lying, but I'll give you my interpretation.

The first four lines state that the word we created, Tao, is not the real name of what we are trying to describe. It's a word humans created because that's how our brains function. Most humans communicate through sounds from our mouths to help with coordination. It's advantageous to do so, after all. However, it's important to remember that objects are not inherently the words we use to describe them.

A book is not a "book." A book is paper, writing, ink, bindings, and more. If I travel to Mexico or France and hold up the object I call "book," those Spanish and French speakers will say different words. Therefore, Tao is not really "Tao." It's much more than that. The names we give objects help us communicate but also limit what the object can mean to us — what the object can become.

In line three, the nameless means things without names — objects or experiences that are not confined by definition or description. Ten thousand things is an ancient Chinese expression for saying "everything." It's like when English speakers might say, "I had to walk one million miles to school each day." We don't mean literally one million miles; we mean a lot of miles. Line four, therefore, means our invention of naming and defining things caused everything else to receive names. Once you begin to describe something, you must describe what it is not. Therefore, what it is not now requires a new name. The process continues forever and will never stop.

Now that we know we can not truly name or define Tao, we move on to what we can do instead. If we are desireless, that is we do not wish to limit or confine the reality of existence to words, our minds are now open to experiences beyond words and our communication abilities. If we desire to define or control Tao, we will only be able to see its effects on us and the world around us, but we won't be able to experience Tao because, as we have stated, Tao is beyond description.

Lines seven through ten explain that desire and desireless come from the same place. The duality of life comes from the same origin, as does everything else. This concept may seem strange or confusing, but modern science shows evidence of this: the Big Bang.

Scientists believe that the entire cosmos started as an infinitely small point and exploded into existence from nothing. Something from nothing. After more years than our mathematics can count, existence will return to nothing. A cycle, pattern, always returning. Darkness within darkness. The ability to experience this concept, not define it, is a pathway in your journey to explore nature and the universe around you. Chapter One of Tao Te Ching explains Tao is everything, yet nothing simultaneously.

Now, let us answer our question. Why does this pattern appear everywhere in nature?

Tao manifests in everything, and everything is a reflection of Tao.

Just as you are your reflection, you are also not your reflection. Your reflection is separate from you, but it is also exactly you. So, too, is Tao in all things. It flows inside them but does not control them. It moves and guides us yet doesn't force us into any circumstance.

The yin-yang is Tao and Tao is yin-yang. When you look at a yin-yang necklace or bumper sticker, you are looking at all of reality. Everything within and without.

This naturally occurring pattern is the universe looking back at itself.

I invite you to take a few moments today to think about this, and I welcome your thoughts and comments. My favorite part about Taoism is that it welcomes interpretations and differences. What is your interpretation of Chapter One or the yin-yang?

# Nothing and Everything All at Once

## ~ Three Self-Identifying Concepts ~

---

*"What I like best is just doing nothing," said Christopher Robin.*

*"How do you do just nothing?" asked Pooh.*

*"Well, it's when grown-ups ask, what are you going to do, and you say nothing. Then, you go out and do it."*

*"I like that," said Pooh. "Let's do that all the time."*

---

I remember watching movies as a kid, but my favorite was "The Many Adventures of Winnie-the-Pooh". By the time I was born in 1982, the film was five years old and had become a staple of pop culture and an instant classic. Growing up, I loved Pooh for his silliness and fun adventures. However, around age 20, I impulse-bought the movie on DVD at Walmart and watched it later that day. While I was ready to relive all the jokes, I was not prepared for the philosophy.

I was not the only person who noticed, either. The year I was born, author Benjamin Hoff also realized the similarities between how Pooh thought about his life and Taoist philosophy. So, Hoff wrote The Tao of Pooh, which stayed on the New York Times bestseller's list for 49 weeks.

## Pu

In his book, Hoff explains how Winnie-the-Pooh represents the Taoist concept, pu, which means "unworked wood; inherent quality; simple." As a child's stuffed bear, Pooh is childlike in his demeanor, honest to a fault, and loving towards everyone, regardless of race or gender. Yes, his favorite friend is the human child Christopher Robin, but most of his adventures occur without him. In other words, Pooh is a bear with little brain. That does not mean Pooh is not smart. Rather, it means he does not concern himself with what he cannot control. He takes on each task as it comes and always moves on when he is naturally able. He does not ponder much beyond what lies before him, and while he worries about his predicaments and feels sad for his friends when they are hurt, Pooh allows those emotions to pass quickly and returns to his natural, simple life.

In Taoism, pu plays a particular part in living life with zìrán, which means to live naturally, spontaneously, and freely. This concept directly leads you to perform your actions with wu wei, meaning without effort. Since I do not want to confuse anyone, let us stop and examine each concept.

## Zìrán

While the meaning of zìrán has changed over time and can change slightly depending on your translation, my interpretation of zìrán is the spontaneity of life. It is a word to describe the natural version of you. When you are born, you are entirely, naturally you. Your mood, emotions, dreams, and actions are not influenced by your parents, society, or preconceived notions. As we grow, we lose this wholeness due to the nature of growing up in a world with rules and definitions.

While we cannot return to having the mind of a baby, we can let go of many distractions and regulations we placed on ourselves. For example, needing to sleep eight hours per night is a rule created for us to work nine-hour shifts. Your body might be different, and each night, depending on your schedule, will be different, too. Trying to force your body to stay awake or asleep can lead to anxiety and stress. However, when I allow myself to be naturally tired or awake, I feel more restful and energetic.

Have you ever thought about who you really are inside? No one can know your mind like you do because no one can be in your head. Zìrán is the "you" that exists when no one else looks and you are completely relaxed.

So, how do we practice returning to this version of ourselves?

## Wu wei

If you have ever played sports, studied for a test, or had fantastic sex, you have experienced wu wei. It is more common than you'd think, but we call it something different in the West. If you are an athlete, you can call it "being in the zone." wu wei is a state of mind you put yourself in to shut out everything else.

Michael Jordan, one of the greatest basketball players of all time, stated that when he was in the zone, he could make every shot and do anything he wanted on the court without trying. It happened effortlessly.

And there lies my favorite translation — effortless action. Action without action. We can perform highly accurate, detailed, complex tasks without stress or strain. Taoists believe you can stay calm, mindful, and peaceful through all your actions, but doing so takes practice.

## Put it all together!

Before you go to bed tonight, place an object by your bed or hang it on a wall so that it is the first thing you see when you wake up. Let this object be a reminder to release any tension you had while you slept. I am a poor sleeper, and my dreams are always nightmares or anxiety-inducing. Having this practice immediately upon opening my eyes allows me to let go of my sleeping mind and return to my waking world refreshed and ready.

Days are not inherently good or bad. Days are simply a passage of time as the Earth turns. The occurrences inside today that you have defined as good or bad cause the day to also take on positive and negative definitions. So, do not tell yourself, "Today is going to be a great day!" Instead, thank the sun for coming back around and be grateful you are a part of this moment. Others will not wake up today, but you did.

Next, take your tasks one at a time and focus as you perform them. When you are getting dressed, only think about getting dressed. When eating breakfast or making coffee, only think about those actions. Make the best cup of coffee you know how. Put on the clothes that speak the loudest to you.

Allow your mind to be simple and accepting as situations arise. You are not a robot, and you will feel anger, sadness, jealousy, and more throughout your life. Trying to live without these emotions is a fool's errand. However, that does not mean we cling to these emotional situations. You can be naturally you and still feel hurt.

As your day goes on, take a moment to breathe. Try to learn the cues your body gives when stressed or hurt. If you recognize when you are headed in one emotional direction, you can accept those feelings, process them, and return to your center. My Taoist coach, George, once told me that life is a highway where you stay on the road. But sometimes, you might find yourself in the ditch and need to turn around to get back on track. In Taoism, we want to practice recognizing when we are in the ditch to return to our journey.

Winnie-the-Pooh might be imaginary, and live only in books and films, but his actions, thoughts, and simple life can teach us to manage ourselves in more calm, relaxing methods through pu, wu wei, and zìrán.

We are walking, talking miracles of nature, and you are perfectly you. Sometimes, we need a little help remembering that. Because if I, a 40-year-old father of three, can use these three concepts to help myself return to who I naturally am, then so can you.

# When Romanizations Go Wrong

## ~ Why Is Tao pronounced Like Dao? ~

Where did Tao with a T come from?

I am often asked, "How do you pronounce Tao? Is it with a T or a D?"

To answer this question, we must travel back to the 1850s. Pretend you travel to China only to discover that you not only have to learn to speak a significantly different tonal language, but you cannot even begin to read written Chinese because they do not use Latin characters. So, what do you do?

你好

If you are Thomas Francis Wade, you begin work on a romanization of the Chinese language. In other words, you turn a phrase like...

...into something Westerners can read: nǐhǎo.

Using Roman (Latin) characters to read and pronounce other languages phonetically is as old as the Romans. The Romans' first known romanization was in Ancient Greece in the first century. Others soon followed, such as Hebrew, Brahmic, and Japanese.

Several romanizations were created throughout history, but none were standardized for traditional Chinese. Wade, however, decided to do so. He spent the rest of his life working on this project with other scholars, such as Herbert Giles and his son, Lionel Giles. By the early 20th century, the Wade-Giles system was in full force in academia and had become the standard romanization for published works.

With this new system, Chinese culture and language reached new audiences and increased its visibility on the world stage. Soon, new students became scholars who passed on their learning to others. Eventually, hundreds of books existed using Wade-Giles.

道

In this Romanization, the character for...

...translated as the way, is spelled Tao because that is what Wade and Giles heard and how they learned to pronounce it.

## Where did Dao with a 'D' come from?

Soon after World War II and another Chinese civil war, the new Chinese Communist Party (CCP) focused on a standardized romanization. Based on previous methods, such as the popular Wade-Giles, the CCP created a similar yet different model. As a tonal language, the new version named Hanyu Pinyin (mostly shorted to simply pinyin) had unique features such as tonal marks above the Latin letters.

For example, Tao became Dào with a tonal mark noting the tonal drop. In a tonal language, not only is your pronunciation important, but the tone of your voice can completely change the phrase's meaning. Adding these marks, like accent marks found in French and Spanish, allowed for a more precise and straightforward method for Westerners to understand Chinese.

The CCP, and the United Nations, quickly adopted pinyin for all government and official Chinese documentation and communications.

## Which one is correct?

Some people, however, were not happy with the new system. Specifically, Taiwan, who adopted Wade-Giles as their official romanization. Governments, schools, and all official communications in Taiwan are still written using the older Wade-Giles method to this day.

The CCP, wanting to show control of an island they claim as their own, has pushed pinyin into the forefront of modern Chinese education, which includes international schools, apps, and online platforms. The CCP also offers certifications for learning Chinese using pinyin. For example, if you've ever used Duolingo to learn Mandarin, you learned pinyin.

## So, how do you pronounce it?

When you hear someone speak Mandarin, the tone their mouth makes is a strong D. Should you talk back to them, but use a T sound as in Tao, they will know what you mean, but you might incur some funny looks in return.

Because most of the translations of Taoist texts were completed decades ago, before pinyin was created, you'll find Tao everywhere. This spelling is prevalent in literature. Scholars, translators, and authors continue to use Wade-Giles because that is how they learned to spell Tao and because of the political implications of accepting the CCP standard.

You will notice I also write the word as Tao, such as The Taoist Online, which is the title of my publication and organization. In creating the name, I debated which romanization to use. I knew using a 'T' would perpetuate the mispronunciation, yet I chose the Wade-Giles spelling due to its uniformity across academic resources, which are easily accessible online.

So, even though I cannot tell you which letter to use when you write Tao, I can tell you which one you should say.

Dao.

# The Tao Is Not Moral

## What is moral?

We need to break down our definitions to understand how the Tao can be good but not moral. First, morality is defined as follows:

*Principles concerning the distinction between right and wrong or good and bad behavior.*

It is important to understand that people create this distinction between what we know as "good" and "bad" actions. These actions are inherently just ACTIONS. What makes them good or bad depends on who performed the action, our relation to the person, and who was on the receiving end of the action. So, in this way, the Tao cannot be moral since it has no notion of right and wrong. In Tao Te Ching chapter 8, Laozi writes,

*The highest good is like water.*

*Water gives life to the ten thousand things and does not strive.*

*It flows in places men reject and so is like the Tao.*

Water nourishes every man, woman, and child regardless of their actions. It does not judge or withhold itself based on what we believe or can accomplish. Water is water, and we use it accordingly.

Such is the Tao. Tao is there, and we are Tao. It runs through everyone and everything and does not withhold itself based on our actions or beliefs. For example, if you were a fish swimming in a stream, the Tao would be the river's water. Predators and prey would all benefit equally, even though predators eat their prey. Your physical actions are can not be classified as good or bad– they are simply actions.

This may shock those who grew up in different religions that teach that their God is moral and just and that there is a specific set of right and wrong actions.

## What is good?

So, by now, I am sure you are thinking, "If the Tao is not moral, how can it be good?"

As I stated at the top, we must return to our definition. As a noun, here is how you can define good:"A benefit or advantage to someone or something."

Aha! Now we're onto something!

---

*It is not morality that makes the Tao good. It is the LACK of morality that makes the Tao good.*

---

Treating all things, and everyone, beneficially and advantageously, just like water, is why the Tao is good... but not moral.

# Knowledge Is Not Always Power

## ~ The More You Grow, the Less You Know ~

### The "joke"

When I was a boy around five years old, my father, who I have not seen in over 20 years, told me a joke.

---

*"Do you know the other name for a Brazil nut?" To which I replied with a simple no. "N***** toes," he said while laughing.*

---

It is amazing how normal the joke seemed to me, contrary to the inexcusable racism which was the reality.

Labels, nicknames, and words. What a useful and horrible tool humans created. On one hand, the ability to effectively communicate hundreds of thousands of ideas, concepts, and perceptions separates us from animals and allows our species to prosper.

On the other hand, however, our words are used to destroy, divide, and separate us into believing one group is better than another. Or that certain things are only one way, when in fact they are not any way at all.

In ancient China, the duality of words was already acknowledged. It is no wonder Laozi, in his Tao Te Ching, the seminal Chinese book of wisdom created over 2,500 years ago, warns against knowledge for knowledge's sake.

## Evidence In Text

The idea that knowledge and definitions can be negative and untrustworthy is not a small line in an otherwise large chapter, but it is repeated throughout the text. For example:

*Abandon wisdom, discard knowledge, and people will benefit a hundredfold. — Tao Te Ching Chapter 19*

*Those who seek knowledge, collect something every day. Those who seek the Way, let go of something every day. — Tao Te Ching Chapter 48*

Also...

*A good person is a bad person's teacher. A bad person is the good person's task. — Tao Te Ching Chapter 27*

*Abandon knowledge and your worries are over. — Tao Te Ching Chapter 19*

## Useless Knowledge

Some readers read these quotes and believe "Oh, Taoism is anti-intellectual." However, read more closely. If that were true, why would Laozi or any other Taoist expert bother writing down anything? They would simply allow their knowledge to die with them.

No, Laozi wanted to share what he had learned, but he's warning us against what I call "useless knowledge", which is knowledge for knowledge's sake. Or, overlearning to the point of using it as a weapon against others.

For example, if you grew up with siblings, it's likely you were part of an argument where the older sibling tried to use your lack of education against you as a way to show dominance. This often occurred in my house with two brothers.

Jeremy and Nicholas would fight, and Jeremy (two years Nicholas' senior) would ask a science question which Nicholas could not answer. Nicholas was not dumb, but his class had not yet covered that topic. Jeremy would use this unanswerable question as a method to prove his superior intelligence.

Did you not grow up with siblings? Turn on the news. Democrats vs. Republicans (for the American readers), black vs. white, LGBTQ+ vs bisexual, and the list goes on and on forever. The more we have used the knowledge we gained about each other, the more we have used it to divide us and hurt each other.

This is why Laozi stated, "Abandon wisdom, discard knowledge, and people will benefit a hundredfold." If we forget about what separates us, then we are only people and we would have to admit how terribly we treat each other. We do not do it because they are simply different, but because we have labeled them into categories which we defined which specific characteristics.

## Mind Blown

In all the lessons, courses, and conversations I have had over the years regarding the Tao, my mind-blown moment came in chapter 27 quoted below.

*What is a good man?*

*A teacher of a bad man.*

*What is a bad man?*

*A good man's charge.*

*If the teacher is not respected,*

*And the pupil not cared for,*

*Confusion will arise, however clever one is.*

*This is the crux of mystery.*

---

In this chapter, if you can live in harmony with the world, you are tasked with showing others. Good cannot be without bad. Confusion, anger, chaos will arise if both good and bad people do not understand this nature. Having useless knowledge will not help in this situation, as the experience of understanding is indescribable.

## When Words Fail

Knowing and experiencing do not equal each other. Knowing about love and experiencing love is not the same.

Do you remember when you fell in love for the first time? Who was it? How old were you? Now, remember the last time you fell in love. Were both of those experiences the same? Probably not. Each love is different and cannot be easily described.

Try to describe how great sex makes you feel. You can describe actions, bodies, and emotions, but you probably cannot describe that sensation which separates the amazing time from the terrible times. You can do the same actions, the same movements, even in the same locations, but "something feels off" when you two do not just "click."

Words are not the end-all be-all for humanity. We do not need more words to divide us, and I hope we finally learn to understand each other.

*We have all the words we will ever need for that.*

# Softness is Life, Hardness is Death

## ~ Allow Yourself To Be Soft ~

Recently, my life has become like an oak tree attempting to stand tall against the raging wind. If the wind blows hard enough, even the mighty oak will snap. Bending to the wind isn't in its nature. Its nature is to stand firm and strong forever. But in Taoism, humans aren't like oak trees. We are a palm tree, able to bend and relax even through the roughest of storms. We may lose leaves and bark, but we don't break because our nature is to survive.

While periods of raging weather often come and go, I feel like there has been more coming and less going lately in my daily journey. Funerals to attend, a house to clean, children to raise, publications to run and edit, websites to build, and finally, working for a company merging into another larger company. And yet, through all the wind, rain, heat, and dust of a Texas summer, I try to remain soft.

Laozi, the legendary author of the Tao Te Ching (the seminal text of Taoism), wrote at great length about softness.

*"Gentleness overcomes strength, softness overcomes hardness." - Chapter 43*

*"People need something they can rely on: highlight your simple self, embrace your original nature, and check your selfishness as you reduce your desires." – Chapter 19*

Laozi preferred to use water as a metaphor for the characteristics of the soft self.

*"The best men (people) are like water, which benefits everything but does not compete with it..." – Chapter 8*

*"Nothing is weaker than water, but there is nothing better than water in overcoming hardships without alternatives. Therefore, weakness prevails over strength, and softness conquers rigidity." – Chapter 78*

Have you ever attended a yoga or tai chi class? The exercises help you learn how to bend, stretch, and strengthen your body through movement. The similarities are not a coincidence but are on purpose.

I attended my weekly online Taoism class with George Thompson who runs wayfinders.global, an online community dedicated to daily practices with our minds and bodies focusing on the Taoist school of thought. It's free to join and I've been a member since it launched a few years ago. Today's lesson was also about softness. In it, he explained when we are alive, our bodies bend and move naturally. Yet, when we die, our bodies grow stiff and harden. Softness means life, while hardness is often associated with death.

So, I invite you to look into your own life. How stiff and rigid have you become? Is it in a belief or a daily activity? Does the thought of changing either cause anxiety or stress? Then, I ask you to try to loosen yourself and your mind through practice. You won't wake up one day and be relaxed all the time because that's not realistic. Instead, the first step is being mindful of your emotions.

Can you realize when you're becoming angry in the moment? If you can stay aware of how you are feeling, and recognize your body signals, then you can practice allowing those emotions to flow out of you. Instead of being stiff and rigid, bend to those emotions, allow yourself to feel them, and let the emotion leave as naturally as it arrived.

Being scared, angry, sad, hurt, are natural and normal states of being. You cannot escape them as long as you are in your physical body. To deny yourself a part of who you are can be damaging not only mentally but physically through higher risks of a stroke, heart attack, depression, anxiety, and more.

One of the most overused, but still useful, phrases I like is "Go with the flow." The saying doesn't mean to allow yourself to be trampled on, it means to move through life without forcing too much. You can't always push through every crowd or win every battle. Going with your natural flow, in harmony with Tao, will allow you to lead a gentler and less abrasive life.

# How To Deal With Hateful Christians

## ~ Or Any Other Religious Debate ~

Christianity and I have a rocky past. Two of my most read articles on Medium discuss how and why I quit Christianity about 10 years ago.

Being a Taoist in north Texas is not easy because Texas bleeds churches. I remember driving down the street to high school and counting the churches I passed on the way. Three. The town my brother lives in currently is more crowded with them. Driving from his house to his church, you must pass a second church, even though his church is less than a mile away!

Since publishing those articles, I have received supportive comments on social media, and on Medium, from concerned Christian readers. They are mostly apologetic and wish my story were different or that I had been treated better. Trust me, so do I.

*Kindness should always be greeted with kindness.*

However, a number of Christian readers made accusations in my comments. Statements like "this was your fault" and "you didn't admit to any wrongdoing which you clearly did" appeared more than once. I also had one comment that asked me to let go of my "baggage."

If you turn on American news now, all you will see is people who claim to be Christians taking away books, civil rights, medical support, and a host of other items because others follow a different standard of living.

So, as a Taoist, what am I to do? Am I supposed to be like a Vulcan in Star Trek and not feel emotions? Should we all become Zen masters and speak in riddles back to them and laugh? The answer might surprise you.

## Tao Te Ching Chapter 56

---

*Those who know do not speak.*

*Those who speak do not know.*

*Seal the openings.*

*Shut the doors.*

*Dull your sharpness.*

*Untie your knots.*

*Dim your light.*

*Become one with the dust.*

*This is called the profound union.*

*Those who obtain it*

*Can neither be seduced nor abandoned.*

*Those who obtain it*

*Can neither be favored nor neglected.*

> *Those who obtain it*
>
> *Can neither be honored nor humiliated.*
>
> *Therefore, they are the most esteemed in the world.*

From the text above the seminal Taoist text, Tao Te Ching, Laozi teaches interfering with a person's true nature is not in harmony with the Tao. We also learn that becoming our true selves is the key to a harmonious life. Everything and everyone on Earth have Tao flowing through it and around it.

People must be allowed to find their own way through life. There is no need to journey into other lands or fight any battles to find your true nature. This quality repeats throughout Tao Te Ching, specifically in chapter 47.

> *Without stepping out the door,*
>
> *You can know the world.*
>
> *Without looking through the window,*
>
> *You can see Heaven's Way.*
>
> *The longer you travel, the less you know.*

Since the ideal person in Taoism is in perfect tune with their nature, they do not need to travel anywhere or speak to anyone.

This is in direct opposition to Jesus' great commission in Matthew 28:19.

*Therefore, go and make disciples of all nations, baptizing them in the name of the Father, and of the Son, and of the Holy Spirit.*

Christianity requires its followers to tell everyone and convince them that "no one comes to the Father (aka heaven) but through Me (Jesus)" (John 14:6).

## The Answer

If you just scrolled to the end, then here is the answer you are looking for. How do you deal with Christians who are combative and mean?

*You do not.*

They are on their own journey, and you cannot know the outcome of their actions and voices as they reverberate through time. As previously discussed, Tao is not moral. It does not judge who is right or wrong. It treats everyone justly, equally, and so should we as members of our communities. When they are sick? Treat them. When they are sad, allow them to cry on your shoulder if they need one.

As mentioned above, Taoists strive for no ambitions and take no credit for rewards. We simply follow the way of water. Treat all people as you do any other person, including those who would do you harm.

# Your Internal Contradictions Contradict Your Internals

## ~ Chatting With a Friend in Need ~

How much do you beat yourself up?

Do you ever feel like you are broken?

Have you ever felt worse about yourself after going to church?

I sure have.

My emotions and mental health have been in terrible conditions throughout my life. I am not an expert on being sad or happy, but I have wisdom to share.

A good friend, Nanie Hurley, asked me a question today inside our Discord community, which touched me. I asked if I could publicly share her question, why she asked, and my response. So, I am thankful she said yes.

Nanie has been seeing a therapist lately and is working through her emotions. Growing up, she was taught to bury or rid herself of negative emotions. Phrases like "Make each day a good one" and "Today is going to be a GREAT day!" have been force-fed to us our entire childhood.

These statements and motivational phrases, among other personal matters, have led to anxiety and doubt. I, too, had these same questions about myself, my beliefs, and my worldview.

*"How does Taoism deal with feelings, emotions, and self-worth?" she asked.*

To answer this question, I focused only on the concept of self-worth as the other two topics, emotions, and feelings, will explain themselves.

Let us compare Taoism to something like Buddhism. There, the Buddha taught that life is suffering and that we can rid ourselves of that suffering through the 8-fold path. However, Taoism teaches there is nothing "wrong" to start with, so attempting to eliminate a part of you would be folly.

For example, how does a tree grow? It grows however it needs to. It can grow sideways or split into parts for it to live. That growth is not wrong or bad; it does not make the tree worthless. It just makes the tree a tree. The tree does what comes naturally and is neither good nor bad. It is itself.

So, now let us look at people. We are also affected by our surroundings (aka family, friends, strangers, environment, etc.), which can cause us to grow into people who do not seem to look or act like anyone else. We are not broken, wrong, or bad. We grew the way we did because that's how people grow. Your "faults" or your self-worth is your second-guessing of your natural state.

But you cannot cut off your arm to cure your hand. You cannot rid yourself of anger, sadness, anxiety, or doubt to always be happy. That is not a natural state.

Humans naturally evolved these different emotions for a reason, and to attempt to reject those parts of you will cause you pain and suffering.

You are you. You are who you grew into being, just as I did. Just as everyone here is doing. That is not to say we cannot learn new things or honor those around us with kindness, love, and harmony with our community.

That is to say, however, we must accept everything about our internal nature. We must accept emotions to pass through us, and when they arise, we must let them go. Just as physical pain arises and we eventually heal, so too can our emotional state heal. But we must learn to accept those feelings and move on from them to return to our natural state of harmony and peace.

*"What you wrote is really interesting because I think I've buried my emotions my whole life,"* she stated.

Most of us, especially in the West, have done the exact same thing. We are told that all negative emotions are bad (from the Devil) and only the positive emotions are good (that is, from God). But how can that be?

Does not believing this teach us that we are broken? I understood that I was broken for decades. I would tell myself, "God must have messed up with me" or ask, "Why can't I fix myself?"

My 11-year-old son got in trouble in school yesterday for lashing out and screaming at another kid. My son had buried his emotions because this kid was picking on him. Eventually, he burst and screamed profanities at him in class. Keeping our emotions inside is so ingrained in our culture that even my child learned it by eleven.

But, in Taoism, you cannot have one without the other. No one can be ONLY happy. We must be sad, angry, and depressed to be happy, pleasant, and joyful.

No ONE without the other. Only together.

My favorite part about Taoism is its openness to my thoughts. Rather than teaching me that my thoughts are broken, Taoism teaches I am me.

I do not have all the answers. I am not well-versed in theology or religion. I am just one person in a room, far from you, dear reader. As we grow, so do our thoughts. Like the tree, we branch out in unusual ways. Some twisted, knotted, and covered in bark. Others are smooth, tall, and straight. Just as your beliefs are not wrong for you, your growth is not wrong either.

Let yourself be who you are. Accept. And then let go.

# The Benefits of True Breathing

I was asked about my daily practice in my training class with George Thompson, but at the time, I did not have a daily practice to speak about. I wanted to, though.

I hate to admit to acting like a stereotype, but I have put on a few pounds as I reached forty and usually enjoy sitting with my phone, tablet, or gaming PC. My kids keep me pretty busy most evenings, especially at the end of the year when our birthdays and holidays hit all at once. But I work from home, so I still sit alone at a computer for 10 hours daily.

It also does not help that I have grown not to like dirt or sweat. On the one hand, it keeps me clean, but on the other hand, it ensures I do not go outside much and avoid most physical labor unless required.

So, when George asked me that question, I had to answer him truthfully. For four years of calling myself a Taoist, my daily practice was all about breathing.

As I have aged, I have grown angrier and more distrustful about the world around me. Anxiety and panic attacks began to take their toll after a cancer scare in 2019, even though it turned out not to be cancer at all.

The final nail in the "perfect health" coffin was tinnitus in 2022. I am not entirely sure what caused it — bacterial infection, loud noises as a teenager and adult, or something else, but I do not understand what silence is anymore. My ears ring like a choir of bells in both ears 24 hours a day, seven days a week.

To combat these health problems, I began to practice 4/7/8 breathing as a method to help me calm down enough to sleep.

You see, I used to lie in bed for 30 minutes, trying to magically fall asleep every night, but with a choir of high-pitched strings in my head that became increasingly difficult. I noticed, however, that if I slowed my heart rate down, I could suddenly fall asleep without having to work at emptying my mind. And miraculously, it worked!

After two months of only three hours of sleep per night, I began to sleep normally again. More than sleeping, 4/7/8 breathing also helped me with anger. I will admit that I am a jealous husband, and my ideas about how spouses should act with their friends while married are dated. Those ideas come from parents who divorced after 30 years and shared those same dated beliefs. Not only were my views of marriage skewed, but my kids tested me to my core. I'm not blind enough to believe "I had it worse" or that "I know how it is to be a kid" because, let's face it, kids face problems I never had to — school shootings, children stolen out of their front yards, a country trying to give up democracy as quickly as possible, and a future they know all too well doesn't hold many bright spots.

So, I did not know how to react, and instead of figuring it out, my response was spanking, yelling, and words. I am a trained public speaker and have studied rhetoric and philosophy my entire life. I know how to circularly argue and prove my point in every situation, even though it is bullshit. My wife and kids eventually discovered the way to "win" arguments were not to engage. Even though I would "win," I was never happy because I knew what they were doing. This toxic behavior eventually led to more stress, anxiety, and frustration about the people who were closest in my life. Luckily, my kids were young, and my wife was patient enough to help see me through the rougher patches.

I write all this because I was hoping you would believe me when I said I needed something to help me in my life or I would lose my mind. Practicing 4/7/8 is simple.

Breathe in for four beats.

Hold for seven beats.

Breathe out for eight beats.

Now, repeat steps one through three until you are comfortable. Like all exercises, it is easier said than done. Some of the friends I have spoken to state it is hard because the practice feels like holding their breath. Others try to replace the word beats with seconds, but holding your breath for seven seconds is tiring when you are angry, and your heart is already trying to beat out of your chest. For me, though, it worked.

After a fight, I would remember to walk away and run 4/7/8 multiple times. Sometimes, I would practice for a minute, while at other times, I would practice one round, which would be enough. After two years of daily breathing practice while trying to sleep with tinnitus and after arguments, I noticed I was able to feel my heart rate beat faster as I became angry. The deep and quick inhalation (four) is followed by a brief pause (seven) and a long exhalation (eight). Not only had I unknowingly forced myself into daily spiritual practice, but I had also mastered it. When an act you practice becomes natural, intuitive, and spontaneous when needed, that's mastery. I was shocked! I noticed I stopped arguing with my wife and kids; I could manage misbehavior or curveballs that life threw my way.

Breathing with 4/7/8 is the first spiritual practice I have ever felt comfortable stating that I mastered, but like all wisdom and mastery, it is only a steppingstone into the next challenge. George soon taught me Taoist True Breathing — a more profound, more powerful technique that 4/7/8 prepares your diaphragm for. In true breathing, your goal is to use your dantian, a spot on your body that is three fingers below your belly button. In Chinese medicine, dantian is a concept that means "field of elixir" or "energy center". It is believed to be a place in the body where energy (qi) is stored and cultivated.

True breathing is also called belly breathing because if you are performing it as intended, your belly should noticeably bulge and contact while your chest should remain mostly still. If you have ever watched a baby sleep, you will notice this is precisely how they breathe — not through their chest, but through their belly. As we age, culture teaches us that having a large belly is undesirable, so we make it as small as possible. When we breathe as adults, we learn how to do so through our chest using only our lungs, limiting the amount of oxygen we can inhale. A snowball rolling downhill effect takes over from here — lower oxygen, shallower breaths, less blood supply for your body, and the cycle continues.

The difference between true breathing and 4/7/8 is that your breathing becomes so slow and shallow that it is imperceptible to feel through your nose as your mouth remains closed. Your heart rate drops dramatically, and eventually, with enough practice, you reach a state of meditation. Without mastering the technique, describing what happens afterward is difficult. Still, from my first few weeks, I can genuinely state that a euphoric feeling washes over me after several minutes. My worries about today fade, and the world around me slows down. The hardest part of the practice is inhaling. As you begin to slow down your breath, you will notice a natural tendency to gasp for air– a sudden feeling of panic when you are out of oxygen.

Mentally fighting this urge to inhale is a key moment to mastering true breathing. "But why? Why do this?" you may ask. "Why does this breathing work for you?" Energy. By returning to our original, natural breathing method, we allow ourselves the capacity to grow and heal many wounds, whether those are mental, physical, or psychological. Growing up, I was taught by my parents that we sleep to regain energy. As you wake up, you will feel relaxed and have enough energy to help you reach the end of your day. However, I have slept several hours many times and felt more tired than when I went to bed. I walked around an amusement park all day and felt more energetic afterwards than when I arrived.

So, if I gain all my energy while sleeping, how can these situations be true? In Taoism, we are taught that your body is an energy factory. Specifically, your dantian is the core of this factory. Like a building that produces cars, movement is required to produce anything. If the factory sat still for hours, no cars would come out.

However, hundreds of vehicles can be made when the building is full of workers, machines, and life. So, too, are our bodies.

We do not gain energy by sitting still; we create energy through movement and practice. The key to turning on our internal energy factory is our breath. If we are not breathing correctly, our exercises will be less efficient, our tension will increase, and anxiety becomes more challenging to overcome.

It is a trick you already mastered but forgot years ago. Remembering takes practice, but you can return to form through the softest, most accessible work you will ever do.

Through my journey, I hope you noticed I am not a role model, and even so, I became a more relaxed and calmer version of myself — a more natural Patrick. I still feel anger, but I do not allow toxic behaviors to run my life anymore. I still cannot control my kids or their lives, but I adapt faster and easier than ever.

Connect with your breathing. As you become stressed or angry, please pay attention to your body signals and try preemptively breathing through them. My 12-year-old son has begun to practice breathing as well. I hope to give him the ability to overcome his internal struggles before they have a chance to take root in his daily routine.

For 40 years, I forgot how to breathe genuinely, and for the next 40 years, I am returning to my center. Find your center.

# Tomorrow Comes Again

Worrying about the past is called regret, while worrying about tomorrow is called anxiety. If you rid yourself of both tomorrow and yesterday, you find that living in the now is much simpler, happier, and healthier. Even though I know this is true, my mind naturally yearns to guess details about tomorrow. Will my career be successful? Will my publications survive and allow other writers to share their dreams and stories? Who knows? I feel as though my whole life has been nothing but a futile attempt to guess the future or reflect on the past. In fact, this entire book follows that pattern more often than not.

However, we can only be who we are, and I can only become who I am becoming. To fight my nature through writing would be to move in disharmony with Tao. Besides, we don't heal in isolation from Tao.

You see, isolation isn't a part of human nature.

One of the core teachings throughout this book is that everything is interconnected and interdependent simultaneously. It sounds contradictory, and it's supposed to.

For a dramatic example, can you wiggle your finger on just one hand? Of course! You can wiggle your toes, fingers, and more, yet those parts can't survive without connecting to the rest of your body. If I cut off my thumb, it will surely die soon after.

Much like your fingers, people need the connectedness of other people. Whether those people are standing in front of them or sitting in a computer chair thousands of miles away, we need to feel like we belong. Humans are, by our nature, communal animals.

Think about how prisons use solitary confinement as punishment. It wouldn't be a punishment if the human mind were naturally conditioned to spend days and weeks without human contact. All of us recently know this to be true. The global pandemic of COVID-19 proved what loneliness can do to our psyche. Weeks of living in an apartment or house, having food delivered, and being unable to leave caused a surge in mental health diagnoses worldwide.

I write to help spread what I've learned about Taoism and myself, but there is much more we can accomplish together!

Living your life in harmony with Tao is as easy as floating along the river and enjoying the bright sun or even the pouring rain. I find it interesting that children enjoy playing in the rain, but as adults we run and hurry to stay dry. If I saw a man in a $500 suit and tie splashing in puddles, I'd probably consider him a fool. But, in chapter 20 of Tao Te Ching, Laotzi states followers of Tao are fools.

*Other have more than they need, but I alone have nothing.*

*I am a fool. Oh, yes! I am confused.*

*Other men are clear and bright,*

*But I alone am dim and weak.*

*Other men are sharp and clever,*

*But I alone am dull and stupid.*

*Oh, I drift like the waves of the sea.*

*Without direction, like the restless wind.*

---

What does this mean? How can you be foolish, yet wise?

As I've already discussed, words fail to convey the true essence of Tao, however, if you and I never meet, I want to leave you with my thoughts on the future and how I pledge to live my life closer to Tao.

On October 27, 2023, at 3:02 AM, the rock I stood on completed its forty-first trip around a giant ball of fire in space during my lifetime. You'd be forgiven for not realizing the event occurred, since the rock didn't notice or seem to care. In fact, most of the other seven billion humans who also happen to inhabit Earth did not notice either.

I spent a good part of my birthday this year the same way I spend every day — in my head, thinking up ways to help myself and others through my writing and my leadership positions. Everyone is a leader in their own way. I co-run my family with my wife and my organization with a fabulous team of editors

As a student of Taoism, I've learned that it's important to speak when you can and stand aside when needed. Speak when you should share your knowledge or experiences, but stay silent when others are speaking. Sounds simple, but I promise it's not. I overstep sometimes, talk out of turn, and raise my voice when inconvenient.

Still, when I guess about the future, I think my life will continue for the next fifteen years with little concern. After those years, my future is relatively blurry. I'll be 56, and my three children will have left the house. My oldest child will turn 30, and my youngest will be 25. I can hardly imagine a world without them at home, but I know it's coming soon.

I reflect on the future, not because I'm anxious, but because I want to emotionally and mentally prepare myself. I used to have nightmares about my mom or family dying, and I would wake up in a panic. The rest of the day, I'd pretend it wouldn't happen for a long time, and I had nothing to worry about, only to relive the same nightmare under a different setting. However, when I started to internalize and accept that the future I saw in my dream was coming one day instead of trying to run from it, my nightmares ended.

Learning to let go of everything I have has become more important the older I've become. This phrase doesn't mean to be an emotionless husk of a human, ignoring all relationships. Instead, the phrase means to guard yourself spiritually and emotionally.

The universe only exists because you do. When you're gone, the universe will end with you, at least from your point of view. But you don't have another point of view outside of your own. So, knowing this, the universe can't exist without you. Those who wish to live forever and see the end of all things will have their wish granted, just not in the way they expected.

If the sky were to open up today and take you away, there would be only you, your actions, and how those actions have affected others. Let those actions speak for you when you're gone. Steve Jobs once said he wanted to leave a dent in the universe, and I try to remember that each day. Through my kids, wife, friends, and writings, I want to leave something behind beyond good deeds and wise words. What actions or words can define me?

As I begin another trip around the sun, I continue with my eyes open and mouth closed. There might be a constant ringing in my ears, but I can still hear the ocean, birds, and wind. I may need glasses, but I can still see the sunshine, pretty flowers, and clouds that look like cotton balls. I may need to rest more during walks, but I can feel the cool grass between my toes, the softness of my wife's skin, and the heat of the concrete on a hot Texas summer day.

Perhaps, in poems, songs and dances, you will find the beauty and peace you deserve. After all, tomorrow comes regardless of your wants or desires. The unknown can be scary, but that's anxiety and fear. Remember, like the swimmer in the river, Tao moves us forward, but it's up to you to choose in which direction you'll swim. There's a saying in theater that when words fail; sing. When singing fails; dance. As a writer, you can sing and dance on the page, but it is called by a different name – poetry.

There's a symmetry in life, but I can't see it.

I have to step away into the ocean, far beyond the shore.

I reach out from that space and grasp nothing.

Only then can I understand.

What is it that whispers in my ear?

I see the full faces of the past return,

but not to me. They return for the new ones,

the young ones, the round pegs in square holes.

I look upon the faces of those yet to come

and see bright days ahead, but the pain remains.

Aging brings wisdom. Youth brings learning.

Slippery slopes of silence steal my soul and

memories meet my mind in time.

Time takes time most of the time.

Sometimes, time tries too hard.

Sometimes, we don't focus on what matters most.

Instead, we focus on foolish follies.

One, Dao; Two, Ying and Yang; Three, the ten thousand things.

Never seeing or controlling anything it controls.

Yet, who controls anything?

Does the bird control its flight?

Does it control the dynamic shape of its wings?

Does it control the force of lift?

It only takes advantage of what is.

I want to know what will be and what's to come

by knowing what happened.

To each their own, they say, so I say, let it rain.

Let it shine until tomorrow is clear, hot,

and sticky like a tabletop near the ocean shore.

Let it pour and pool until I tread water.

Let it drown my future in a dark and hazardous mist.

I revel in the unknown and enjoy the haze.

Tomorrow comes again.

# Acknowledgements

I would like to express my deepest gratitude to my editor, Nanie Hurley. Without her guidance, support, and editorial prowess, this book would not have been possible or as good as it became.

I offer my most sincere gratitude to Nathan Welsh and Simon Kupfer who took a risk by joining The Taoist Online extremely early and kick-started the organization.

I would like to thank Robin Wilding, whose investigative insight, late-night rants, and political clout in the Medium community opened doors that would have otherwise remained closed.

I offer my gratitude to Debra G. Harmen MEd. for her recommendation to join the Medium Boost Nomination Pilot program. Without this program's membership, the organization would not have had the rapid growth and I would not have had the finances to fund the organization early on.

# About the Author

Patrick Stewart lives in Fort Worth, Texas, with his wife and three kids. He has a full-time job in the tech industry, and somehow, he still finds the energy to run The Taoist Online, his online organization; help other writers and readers; write articles, newsletters, books; and record podcasts and YouTube videos. Patrick doesn't share the secret to the 100-hour day.

Read more at https://thetaoistcorner.net.